50 Fermentation Recipes:

The Beginner's Cookbook to Fermented Eating

Includes 50 Recipes!

Disclaimer and Terms of Use:

Table of Contents

Introduction

Today, the market is flooded with numerous high-sodium preserved products that offer no nutritional value and no health benefits. These products are cheap and are slightly delicious, but those are the only benefits that you will receive from these food. What if I told you that you can still enjoy preserved foods at a low cost, and receive some of the best health benefits that food as to offer? Well, that is what this book is all about.

In this book, *50 Fermentation Recipes:* *The Beginner's Cookbook to Fermented Eating* you will be opened up to the world of fermented, cured, and preserved foods. You will discover how to make these food from the comfort of your own home, and in return discover that you can save money by doing things all on your own.

Fermentation involves the process of food preservation, which in return increases the nutrient content of the food. This happens when the natural bacteria found in foods break down the rudiments of the food to make it easier to digest, and much more nutritious. Isn't it great to know that you are giving your body the best nutrients and care every day? Consuming these fermented and natural foods will give you the nutrients your body needs and will increase your chances of reaching optimal heath.

Fermented Vegetables

Cultured Broccoli Salad

Yield: Four Quarts
Active Time: 10 minutes
Fermenting Time: 3 Days
Total Time: 3 Days, 10 minutes

Ingredients
1 cup raisins
1 cup grapes
1 large red onion, thinly sliced
2 heads of broccoli (cut into florets)
4 medium carrots, shredded
4 tsp lemon juice, freshly squeezed
1 cup kefir whey
3 tsp Himalayan Pink salt
Chlorine-free, filtered water

Tools
Two (½ Gallon) fermenting jars with airlock lid
One large bowl

Methods
1. In a large bowl, combine broccoli, raisins, grapes, onion, carrots, and salt into a large bowl. Mix well to combine the ingredients.
2. Divide the vegetable mixture into two equal portions and add each portion to each of the fermenting jars.
3. Add the lemon juice and kefir whey to the jar and cover all the ingredients with water, leaving about 1 to 2 inches of space in the jar for the lid to close without contents of the jar overflowing. Place jars onto a surface that is hidden from direct sunlight for a minimum of 3 days.

4. Be sure to check the jars every day to be sure that the vegetables remain fully submerged into the water. If the vegetables begin to rise, gently push them down so that they remain below the surface of the water.
5. If you see any white spots in the jar, this is okay. You should remove the vegetables that have white spots on them and press the remaining vegetables back below the surface of the water.
6. After 3 days remove the vegetables and enjoy your delicious, cultured, broccoli salad. Place the reminder into the refrigerator.

Cultured Green Beans

Yield: One Quart
Active Time: 10 minutes
Fermenting Time: 3 Days
Total Time: 3 Days, 10 minutes

Ingredients
1 pound fresh green beans, tailed, washed, and chopped
2 garlic cloves
½ cup kefir whey
2 tsp dill seeds
1 tsp black peppercorns
1 tsp Himalayan Pink salt
Chlorine-free, filtered water

Tools
One (1-Quart) fermenting jar with airlock lid
One large bowl

Methods
1. Add green beans, garlic, and dill seeds, and salt to the large bowl. Mix well until the ingredients are well combined. Add the vegetables to the fermenting jar.
2. Add the kefir whey to the jar and cover all of the ingredients with water, leaving about 1 to 2 inches of space in the jar for the lid to close without contents of the jar overflowing. Place jars onto a surface that is hidden from direct sunlight for a minimum of 3 days.
3. After 3 days, enjoy your cultured vegetables and place the remainder into the fridge.

Fermented Garlic and Radishes

Yield: One Half-Quart
Active Time: 10 minutes
Fermenting Time: 3 to 7 days
Total Time: Up to 7 days, 10 minutes

Ingredients
3 ½ cup radishes
3 garlic cloves
3 tbsp Himalayan Pink salt
4 cups chlorine-free, filtered water

Tools
One (1 ½-quart) fermenting jar with airlock lid
One small bowl
One clean kitchen towel
One small weight (For example, fill plastic bag about halfway full with water. This will be used to keep the ingredients compressed during fermentation.)

Method
1. In the small bowl, mix together salt and water. Stir until the salt is dissolved.
2. Add the radishes to the and garlic to the fermenting jar, and pour the salt water over the vegetables, leaving about 1 to 2 inches of space in the jar for the lid to close without contents of the jar overflowing. Place the weight inside the mouth of the jar, and cover with the lead.
3. Drape the kitchen towel around the jar and place jars onto a surface that is hidden from direct sunlight for a minimum of 3 days to 7 days.

4. After the vegetables are ready, remove the weight and enjoy your cultured vegetables and place the remainder into the fridge.

Pickled Garlic Scapes

Yield: One Quart
Active Time: 5 minutes
Fermenting Time: 2 to 7 days
Total Time: 2 to 7 days, 5 minutes

Ingredients
1 quart garlic scapes, trimmed
1 package vegetable starter culture
1 quart chlorine-free, filtered water
1 ½ tsp Himalayan Pink salt

Tools
One (4-quart) fermenting crock

Method
1. Add the garlic scapes to the fermenting crock
2. Mix together starter culture, salt, and water in a large bowl. Mix until the salt and starter culture are dissolved, and pour over the garlic scapes. Be sure that the scapes are completely submerged under the salt and culture mixture. Cover the pot.
3. Place the fermenting crock onto a surface that is hidden from direct sunlight, and allow to ferment for a minimum of 2 to 7 days.
4. Store remaining scapes in an airtight container in the fridge.

Spicy Kimchi Pickles

Yield: One Quart
Active Time: 20 minutes
Fermenting Time: Up to 5 days
Total Time: Up to 5 days, 20 minutes

Ingredients
6 cucumbers, partially cleaned, quartered, and seeds removed (do not peel)
4 ramps or green onions, bulbs removed and cut into ½" pieces
2 tbsp red chili pepper powder
1 ½ tbsp Himalayan Pink salt

Tools
One (1-quart) fermenting jars with airlock lid
One large bowl

Method
1. Cut the quartered cucumbers into ¾" pieces, and place them into the large bowl. Sprinkle with salt. Mix well to distribute the salt, and allow the cucumbers to sit for about 7 to 10 minutes.
2. When ready rinse and drain the cucumbers. Return the cucumbers to the bowl. Add onions and chili powder. Toss well to combine.
3. Add to the fermenting jar and press the vegetables down lightly and cover with lid.
4. Place jar onto a surface that is hidden from direct sunlight, and allow to ferment for up to 5 days.
5. After about one day, mix together 1 tablespoon of water to the fermenting jar and replace the lid.

6. After the vegetables are ready, enjoy and place the remainder into the fridge.

Tomatillo Sauerkraut

Yield: Two Quarts
Active Time: 15 minutes
Sweating Time: 30 to 60 minutes
Fermenting Time: 10 to 21 days
Total Time: Up to 21 days, 1 hour, and 15 minutes

Ingredients
3 pounds green cabbage, shredded
1 pound tomatillos, husks removed and halved
1 cup fresh cilantro, roughly chopped
1 ½ tbsp ground coriander
2 ½ tbsp Himalayan Pink salt

Tools
One (1-gallon) glass jar with lid
One large bowl
One plastic gallon bag
One clean kitchen towel

Method
1. Add cabbage and salt to the large bowl. Mix well to distribute the salt throughout the cabbage. Set the cabbage to the side and allow to sweat for a minimum of 30 to 60 minutes.
2. After the cabbage is ready, mix in the tomatillos, coriander, and cilantro. Toss well to combine. Add all of the ingredients to the glass jar. Press the ingredients down firmly into the jar. Add the weight to allow as much liquid as possible to be released from the vegetables.
3. Once you are done releasing the liquid from the vegetables, there should be enough liquid

to cover them by an inch or so. If you are not able to accomplish this, add chlorine-free, filtered water as needed.

4. Place the gallon bag into the jar, with the bottom side touching the cabbage. Press down, and allow the opening of the bag to hang over the top. Fill the bag with water, to allow the bag to take the shape of the jar. Cover with the kitchen towel.

5. Place jar onto a surface that is hidden from direct sunlight, and allow to ferment for up a minimum of 10 to 21 days.

6. After the vegetables are ready, enjoy and place the remainder into the fridge.

Fermented Radishes & Brussels Sprouts

Yield: One and One-half Quart
Active Time: 1 hour
Fermenting Time: 7 to 10 days
Total Time: 7 to 10 days, 1 hour

Ingredients
36 Brussels sprouts, halved
36 radishes, thinly sliced
1 large yellow onion, thinly sliced
4 cups chlorine-free, filtered water
3 tbsp Himalayan Pink salt

Tools
One (1 ½-quart) fermenting jar with airlock lid
One large bowl

Method
1. Add all of the vegetables to the fermenting jar and press down onto the vegetables very firmly to compact them and set them to the side.
2. In a large bowl, combine water and salt. Pour the brine into the fermenting jar. Be sure that the vegetables are fully submerged beneath the brine. If not, then add more water as needed. Cover with lid.
3. Place jar onto a surface that is hidden from direct sunlight, and allow to ferment for up a minimum of 7 to 10 days.
4. After the vegetables are ready, enjoy and place the remainder into the fridge.

Pickled Jalapeños

Yield: One Quart
Active Time: 10 minutes
Fermenting Time: 5 to 7 days
Total Time: 5 to 7 days, 10 minutes

Ingredients
1 quart fresh jalapeños, sorted and rinsed
1 medium yellow onion, sliced
4 garlic cloves
1 quart chlorine-free, filtered water
3 tbsp Himalayan Pink salt

Tools
Two (1-quart) fermenting jars with airlock lid
One large bowl

Method
1. Add the and even portion of peppers, garlic, and onion to each of the fermenting jars. Set to the side.
2. In a large bowl, combine water and salt. Mix well until the salt is dissolved.
3. Pour and even portion of the salt water into each of the vegetable-filled fermenting jars. Ensure that the vegetables are well submerged beneath the salt water, and cover with the lid.
4. Place jars onto a surface that is hidden from direct sunlight, and allow to ferment for a minimum of 5 to 7 days.
5. After the vegetables are ready, enjoy and place the remainder into the fridge.

Zucchini Pickles

Yield: One Quart
Active Time: 10 minutes
Fermenting Time: 3 days
Total Time: 3 days, 10 minutes

Ingredients

3 medium zucchinis, partially cleaned and cut into ¼"
thick slices (do not peel)
2 tbsp kefir whey
8 garlic cloves, minced
2 cups chlorine-free, filtered water
½ cup fresh basil, rinsed and roughly chopped
2 tbsp Himalayan Pink salt

Tools

One (1-quart) fermenting jar with airlock lid
One large bowl

Method

1. Layer the zucchinis, garlic, and basil in even layers inside of the fermenting jar. Set to the side.
2. In a large bowl, mix together water, whey, and salt. Stir until the whey and salt are completely dissolved and pour over the vegetables in the fermenting jar.
3. Be sure that the brine completely covers the vegetables. Leave about 1 to 2 inches of space in the jar for the lid to close without contents of the jar overflowing. Place jars onto a surface that is hidden from direct sunlight for a minimum of 3 days.
4. Be sure to check the jars every day to be sure that the vegetables remain fully submerged

into the water. If the vegetables begin to rise, gently push them down so that they remain below the surface of the water.

5. Store the remainder in the fridge.

Fermented Yogurts

Black and Blue Kefir

Yield: 2 cups
Active Time: 5 minutes
Blending Time: 5 minutes
Total Time: 5 minutes

Ingredients
½ cup blueberries
½ cup blackberries
1 cup kefir
1 tbsp coconut sugar

Tools
Blender

Method
1. Add all of the ingredients to the blender and blend the ingredients for a minimum of 2 to 5 minutes.
2. Enjoy as desired!

Probiotic Coconut Yogurt

Yield: 16 ounces
Active Time: 10 minutes
Blending Time: 5 minutes
Fermenting Time: 16 hours
Total Time: 15 minutes

Ingredients
¾ cup organic raw coconut water
1 ½ cup organic raw coconut meat
2 tbsp probiotic powder

Tools
Food Processor
One (1-quart) fermenting jar with airlock lid

Method
1. Add all of the ingredients into the food processor and pour into the fermenting jar. Cover with the lid.
2. Place jar onto a surface that is hidden from direct sunlight, and allow to ferment for a minimum of 16 hours.
3. When ready to serve, feel free to add anything you would like to the yogurt.

Almond Yogurt

Yield: Four Quarts
Active Time: 35 minutes
Fermenting Time: 14 to 20 hours
Total Time: 14 to 20 hours, 35 minutes

Ingredients
2 quarts almond milk
3 tbsp fruit pectin
6 tbsp honey (divided)
Yogurt culture
2 tbsp vanilla extract
⅛ cup chlorine-free, filtered water

Tools
One large saucepan
One small saucepan
Two (2-quart) fermenting jars with airlock lid
Yogurt Maker

Method
1. In a large saucepan, heat the coconut milk to about 180 degrees to sterilize the milk. Remove the milk from the heat and allow to cool to about 105 degrees, and pour into a large glass jar. Set about one cup of the coconut milk to the side.
2. Add the cultures and 2 tablespoons honey to the one cup of milk, and pour into the large glass of milk.
3. Add the coconut milk mixture to a yogurt maker, and brew the coconut milk for a minimum of 8 to 12 hours.

4. Remove the coconut milk mixture from the yogurt maker, and set to the side.
5. In a small pot, add the water and bring to a boil over medium heat. Stir in vanilla extract, remaining honey and fruit pectin. Mix until the mixture is well blended. Remove from heat and add to the coconut milk mixture. Pour into 2 quart jars.
6. Place in the fridge to chill and ferment for a minimum of 6 to 8 hours, or until the yogurt has separated.
7. Serve immediately.

Fermented Meats

Cured Corned Beef

Yield: Ten Servings
Active Time: 10 minutes
Curing Time: 5 to 10 days
Total Time: Up to 10 days, 10 minutes

Ingredients
3 pounds beef brisket, rinsed and patted dry
2 cups whey
2 cups celery juice
½ cup pickling spices
½ cup Himalayan Pink salt

Tools
One Cotton cheesecloth
One Cotton cooking twine
One large ceramic bowl with a lid
One ceramic plate (or any other weight)
One Medium bowl

Method
1. In a medium bowl, mix together pickling spice and salt, and rub the mixture all over the brisket. Tightly roll the brisket and tie it together using the cotton twine. Wrap the brisket up tightly in the cheesecloth.
2. Place the wrapped beef brisket into the ceramic bowl, and pour the fresh whey and celery juice over the beef. The beef brisket should be fully submerged into the liquid. If the brisket does not appear to be beneath the surface of the celery juice mixture, add water as needed.
3. Place the ceramic plate on top of the brisket to weight it down. Cover the bowl with the lid.

4. Cure the beef on in the fridge for a minimum of 5 to 10 days. Turn the meat each day so ensure an even cure.
5. When ready to enjoy, drain the liquid and serve the beef as you prefer.

Fermented Kosher Apple Salami Sausages

Yield: 3 Pounds
Active Time: 15 minutes
Fermenting Time: 3 days
Drying Time: 2 to 3 months
Total Time: 2 to 3 months, 3 days, and 15 minutes

Ingredients
2 pounds beef chuck
4 large green apples, peeled, cored, and shredded
1 tbsp Marsala white wine
1 tsp smoked paprika
½ tsp dextrose (0.2%)
½ tsp whey
2 tbsp freeze-dried cilantro
1 tbsp garlic powder
2 tsp ground white pepper
5 tsp Himalayan Pink salt
1 cup beef tallow or brisket fat

Tools
Meat grinder
One large bowl
3-inch protein-lined fibrous meat casings
Cold smoker

Methods
1. Grind the meat through the meat grinder and dump the meat into the large bowl.
2. Add the remaining ingredient to the bowl, and with clean hands combine and work through the meat.

3. Stuff the meat into the casings, and ferment in a cool, dry place for a minimum of 3 days. Be sure the environment is at about 68 degrees.
4. When the meat is ready cold smoke the meat for a minimum of 4 days.
5. Dry the sausages for about 2 to 3 months at about 60 degrees.
6. When ready to serve, enjoy the sausages as desired and store the remainder in the fridge.

Spicy Dry Sheep Sausages

Yield: 2 Pounds
Active Time: 1 hour
Fermenting Time: 27 to 37 days
Smoking Time: 2 to 3 days
Total Time: 29 to 40 days, 1 hour

Ingredients
1 ¾ pound sheep meat with the connective tissue, cut into 1" thick pieces
¼ pound lean beef, cut into 1" thick pieces
2 garlic cloves, minced
1 tsp 100% pure cane sugar
1 tsp pickling spices
2 tbsp cayenne pepper
1 tsp freshly ground black pepper
5 tsp Himalayan Pink salt
⅛ cup beef tallow

Tools
Meat grinder
One large bowl
3-inch protein-lined fibrous meat casings
Cold smoker

Method
1. In the large bowl, mix together pickling spices, salt, sugar, and beef tallow. Add the meat pieces and combine all of the ingredients using clean hands.
2. Grind the meat through the meat grinder and stuff the meat into the casing.
3. Section off the sausages and hang them up to cure for a minimum of 5 to 7 days.

4. Add the sausages to the cold smoker, and smoke them for a minimum of 2 to 3 days.
5. Remove the sausages from the cold smoker and hang them up to dry for a minimum of 5 to 7 days at 60 degrees with a humidity of 80 to 84%.
6. After that, check the sausages and continue to dry them for about 20 to 23 days at 54 degrees at 74 to 78% humidity.
7. When ready to serve, enjoy the sausages as desired and store the remainder in the fridge.

Fermented Herring

Yield: One Liter
Active Time: 5 minutes
Fermenting Time: 3 to 5 days
Total Time: 3 to 5 days, 5 minutes

Ingredients
4 fresh Herring fillets, skin, bones removed, and chopped
1 large white onion
4 tbsp kefir whey
½ liter chlorine-free, filtered water
10 bay leaves
¼ cup fresh dill, roughly chopped
½ tsp coriander seed
1 tsp black peppercorns
1 tbsp Himalayan Pink salt

Tools
One (1-liter) fermenting jar with airlock lid
One large bowl

Method
1. Add fish, onions, coriander, bay leaves, onions, and dill to the jar. Set to the side.
2. In a large bowl, combine water salt, and whey. Mix well until the salt and whey are dissolved and pour into the fermenting jar. Be sure the ingredient are well submerged into the brine. Add more water as needed and cover with lid.
3. Place jar onto a surface that is hidden from direct sunlight, and allow to ferment for up a minimum of 3 to 5 days.
4. After the fish and vegetables are ready, enjoy and place the remainder into the fridge.

Spicy Pickled Hotdogs

Yield: Two Quarts
Active Time: 20 minutes
Cooking Time: 10 minutes
Fermenting Time: 2 to 3 days
Total Time: Up to 3 days, 30 minutes

Ingredients
16 beef hot dogs, halved
4 garlic cloves
3 cups hot banana peppers
2 cups white vinegar
2 cups chlorine-free, filtered water
2 cups 100% pure cane sugar
½ tbsp alum
1 ½ tbsp pickling spice

Tools
Two (1-quart) fermenting jars with airlock lid
One tall, large saucepan
One large saucepan

Method
1. Evenly layer the hotdogs, peppers, and garlic in both of the fermenting jars, with the hotdogs being the first layer and the peppers being the second layer. Continue until each jar is full. Set to the side.
2. In the large bowl, combine water, vinegar, sugar, alum, and pickling spice in a large saucepan. Stirring constantly, bring to a boil over medium-high heat, allowing the sugar to dissolve. Remove from heat and allow to cool.
3. Add and even amount of the brine to each of the fermenting jars, leaving about ½" to ¾" of

space from the top of the jar. All of the ingredients should be fully submerged beneath the brine, if not add more water as needed. Close the jars. Set to the side.

4. Fill the tall saucepan about halfway full with water. Bring to a boil and immediately place the jars into the pot. Allow to boil for about 5 minutes. Remove from the heat, let the jars sit in the water for an additional 10 minutes.

5. Remove the jars from the pot and allow them to cool. You can enjoy the hotdogs right away or allow them to sit in the fridge for about 2 to 3 days before eating.

Fermented Condiments

Lacto-Fermented Mayonnaise

Yield: One Cup
Active Time: 10 minutes
Fermenting Time: 8 hours
Total Time: 8 hours, 10 minutes

Ingredients
1 free-range egg
1 free-range egg yolk
1 tbsp liquid whey
1 tsp Dijon mustard
2 tbsp lemon juice, freshly squeezed
⅛ tsp cayenne pepper
1 tsp Himalayan Pink salt
1 cup unrefined extra-virgin coconut oil, melted

Tools
One (8-ounce) fermenting jar with airlock
Food processor

Method
1. Combine all ingredients except the oil into the food processor and blend for a minimum of 30 seconds.
2. Remove the air cap from the lid of the food processor and continue blending while simultaneously pouring the coconut oil inside. Continue this until the mixture becomes fluffy.
3. Pour into the fermenting jar, and cover with lid.
4. Place the jar onto a surface that is hidden from direct sunlight, and allow the mayo to ferment for a minimum of 8 hours.
5. When ready to serve, enjoy the mayo with your favorite dish and place the remainder into the freezer.

Horseradish Sauce

Yield: One Cup
Active Time: 10 minutes
Fermenting Time: 3 to 7 days
Total Time: 3 to 7 days, 10 minutes

Ingredients
1 cup fresh horseradish root, peeled and chopped
1 package vegetable starter culture
¼ cup chlorine-free, filtered water
1 ½ Himalayan Pink salt

Tools
Blender
One (8-ounce) fermenting jar with airlock lid

Method
1. Add horseradish, starter culture, and salt to the blender. Pulse for a minimum of 1 to 2 minutes, or until the ingredients are well combined. Discontinue blending.
2. Add water to the horseradish mixture, and continue blending for another 3 to 4 minutes, or until the ingredients form a smooth paste. If needed, add more water to the paste.
3. Add the horseradish to the fermenting jar and top-off with a little water. Cover with lid, and allow the horseradish sauce to ferment on a surface that is hidden from direct sunlight for a minimum of 3 to 7 days. Enjoy the sauce with your favorite dish and store the remaining sauce in the fridge.

Beetroot and Apple Relish

Yield: Four Quarts
Active Time: 20 minutes
Fermenting Time: 3 to 4 days
Total Time: 3 to 4 days, 20 minutes

Ingredients
3 large green apples, cored and shredded
3 large beets, peeled and shredded
1 package vegetable starter culture
2 star anise pods
1 tbsp whole cloves
1 tbsp Himalayan Pink salt

Tools
Two (2-quart) fermenting jars with airlock lid
One large bowl

Method
1. In the large bowl, combine apples, beets, star anise, and cloves. Toss until the ingredients are well combined.
2. Add layer even portions of the apple mixture to each of the fermenting jars, topping each layer with an even serving of salt and vegetable culture.
3. Press the veggies down into the jar with a wooden spoon to encourage the vegetables.
4. Place jars onto a surface that is hidden from direct sunlight, and allow to ferment for a minimum of 3 to 4 days.
5. After the vegetables are ready, enjoy and place the remainder into the fridge.

Fermented Hot Pepper Sauce

Yield: One Quart
Active Time: 10 minutes
Fermenting Time: 5 days
Total Time: 5 days, 10 minutes

Ingredients
2 Poblano peppers, stems removed
2 Jalapeño peppers, stems removed
1 Habanero pepper, stem removed
2 dried chipotle peppers, soaked
3 large red cayenne peppers, stems removed
3 garlic cloves
1 tbsp tomato paste
2 cups chlorine-free, filtered water
1 tbsp distilled white vinegar
2 ½ tbsp Himalayan Pink salt

Tools
One (1-quart) fermenting jar with airlock lid
One small bowl
Food Processor
Goggles
Gloves

Method
1. Before you begin handling the peppers, be sure to put on gloves and goggles to protect eyes and hands.
2. Add peppers, garlic, tomato paste, and vinegar to the food processor. Remove the lid and sprinkle pepper mixture with ½ tablespoon salt. Stir to evenly distribute the salt throughout the pepper mixture. Replace the lid and allow the

pepper puree to sit for a minimum of 1 hour to allow the juices to release.

3. Press the mixture down using a wooden spoon to release more of the water.
4. In a small bowl, mix together water and remaining salt. Set to the side.
5. Pour the pepper puree into the fermenting jar, and top-off with brine. Be sure that the pepper mixture is at 1 inch beneath the surface of the water. Add water as needed.
6. Place jar onto a surface that is hidden from direct sunlight, and allow to ferment for up a minimum of 5 days.
7. After the peppers are ready, enjoy and place the remainder into the fridge.

Fermented Sweet and Tangy Sauce

Yield: 2 cups
Active Time: 10 minutes
Fermenting Time: 5 days
Total Time: 5 days, 10 minutes

Ingredients
¼ cup tahini
¼ cup tamari
¼ cup organic raw honey
3 garlic cloves
¼ cup nutritional yeast
¼ cup chlorine-free, filtered water
⅓ cup unrefined extra-virgin olive oil

Tools
Blender
One (16-ounce) fermenting jar

Method
1. Add all of the ingredients to the blender, and blend until a smooth consistency is reached. Pour the tahini mixture into the fermenting jar.
2. Place jar onto a surface that is hidden from direct sunlight, and allow to ferment for up a minimum of 5 days.
3. When ready to serve, enjoy the sauce with your favorite dishes. Place the remainder into the fridge.

Fiery Fermented Pepper Salsa

Yield: One Quart
Active Time: 10 minutes
Fermenting Time: 2 to 3 days
Cooking Time: 20 minutes
Total Time: 2 to 3 days, 30 minutes

Ingredients
5 jalapeño peppers, stems removed
5 Anaheim peppers, stems removed
7 small sweet bell peppers, stems removed (any color)
3 Poblano peppers, stems removed
4 large heirloom tomatoes, chopped
7 garlic cloves
1 cup fresh cilantro, roughly chopped
¼ cup sauerkraut juice
¼ tsp whey
1 tbsp Himalayan Pink salt

Tools
One (1-quart) fermenting jar with airlock lid
One large baking sheet
Food Processor
Aluminum foil

Methods
1. Set oven to 450 degrees, and line the large baking sheet with aluminum foil.
2. Arrange the peppers in a single layer onto the prepared baking sheet, and place in the oven to char for a minimum of 20 minutes, or until the peppers blister and slightly burn. Remove from oven and allow the peppers to cool.

3. Once the peppers are cooled, add them to the food processor along with the remaining ingredients. Process until mixture is smooth, but slightly chunky. Pour into the fermenting jar.
4. Place jar onto a surface that is hidden from direct sunlight, and allow to ferment for up a minimum of 2 to 3 days.
5. After the peppers are ready, enjoy and place the remainder into the fridge.

Lacto-Fermented Ketchup

Yield: 2 cups
Active Time: 10 minutes
Fermenting Time: 5 days
Total Time: 5 days, 10 minutes

Ingredients
2 cups tomato paste
2 tsp fish sauce
2 tbsp apple cider vinegar
¼ cup organic raw honey
¼ cup kefir whey
¼ tsp ground cinnamon
⅛ tsp cayenne pepper
¼ tsp ground cloves
1 tsp Himalayan Pink salt

Tools
One large bowl
One (20-ounce) fermenting jar with airlock lid

Method
1. In the large bowl, mix together all ingredients until well blended and combined.
2. Pour into the fermenting jar, and place jar onto a surface that is hidden from direct sunlight, and allow to ferment for up a minimum of 5 days.
3. Enjoy with your favorite dishes and store the remainder in the fridge.

Spicy Pickled Slaw

Yield: One Quart
Active Time: 20 minutes
Fermenting Time: 3 days
Total Time: 3 days, 20 minutes

Ingredients
2 bunches of radish, rinsed and shredded
5 large carrots, rinsed, peeled, and shredded
3 fresh jalapeños, sliced (or to taste)
½ cup distilled white wine vinegar
¼ cup apple cider vinegar
½ cup 100% pure cane sugar
¼ cup fresh cilantro, roughly chopped
Himalayan Pink salt, to taste

Tools
One medium saucepan
One (1-quart) fermenting jar with airlock lid

Methods
1. Add vegetables to the fermenting jar and press down. Set to the side.
2. In the medium saucepan, bring all of the vinegars and sugar to a boil. Stir constantly. Once sugar is dissolved, remove from heat and allow the vinegar mixture to cool to room temperature.
3. Once the vinegar mixture is cooled pour it into the fermenting jar.
4. Place jar onto a surface that is hidden from direct sunlight, and allow to ferment for up a minimum of 3 days.
5. After the vegetables are ready, enjoy and place the remainder into the fridge.

Fermented Fruits

Lime Pickles

Yield: Seven Cups
Active Time: 15 minutes
Fermenting Time: 5 to 6 weeks
Total Time: 5 to 6 weeks, 15 minutes

Ingredients
18 fresh limes, cut into eighths
1 tbsp distilled white vinegar
½ cup mustard seeds
¼ cup fenugreek seeds, crushed
3 tbsp turmeric
1 tbsp asofoetida
3 tbsp cayenne pepper
4 tbsp Himalayan Pink salt
1 cup unrefined extra-virgin olive oil

Tools
One (½-gallon) fermenting jar or regular glass jar with lid
One large bowl

Method
1. Add limes, turmeric, salt, and vinegar to the large bowl. Mix well to combine and coat the limes. Add to the fermenting jar, and cover with the lid.
2. Place jar onto a surface that is hidden from direct sunlight, and allow to ferment for up a minimum of 4 weeks, stirring every tree days.
3. After the limes have fermented for about 4 weeks, add the olive oil, mustard seeds, asofoetida, fenugreek, and cayenne pepper to the fermenting jar. Cover with the lid.

4. Return the jar to the fermenting surface and allow to side for an additional 2 weeks.
5. After the vegetables are ready, enjoy and place the remainder into the fridge.

Moroccan Preserved Lemons

Yield: 2 ½ Pounds
Active Time: 30 minutes
Fermenting Time: 4 weeks
Total Time: 4 weeks, 30 minutes

Ingredients
2 ½ pounds lemons, tips removed (**Important:** Avoid cutting into the flesh!)
¼ Himalayan Pink salt

Tools
One (4-quart) fermenting crock

Method
1. Keeping the lemons together at the base, quarter the lemons and sprinkle and even amount of salt into each of the lemons.
2. Add the lemons to the fermenting crock, and mash the down with a wooden spoon to soften the peels and release juices.
3. Continue the mashing and adding salt until the lemons are submerged beneath the juices.
4. Place jar onto a surface that is hidden from direct sunlight, and allow to ferment for up a minimum of 4 weeks, stirring every tree days.
5. After the lemons are ready, enjoy and place the remainder into the fridge. Has a shelf life of up to 2 years.

Cranberry Chutney

Yield: 3 Cups
Active Time: 10 minutes
Fermenting Time: 2 days
Total Time: 2 days, 10 minutes

Ingredients
3 cups fresh cranberries
½ cup pecans, roughly chopped
½ cup raisins
½ cup kefir whey
½ organic raw honey
½ cup apple juice
1 tbsp lemon juice, freshly squeezed
1 tbsp orange juice, freshly squeezed
1 tsp ground cinnamon
1 tsp Himalayan Pink salt

Tools
One large bowl
One (1-quart) fermenting jar with airlock lid
Blender

Method
1. Combine cranberries, pecans, honey, apple juice, lemon juice, orange juice, cinnamon, whey, and salt into a large blender. Blend until the desired consistency is reached.
2. Pour the contents of the blender into the large bowl and gently fold in the raisins. Transfer to the fermenting jar and cover with lid.
3. Place jar onto a surface that is hidden from direct sunlight, and allow to ferment for up a minimum of 2 days.
4. Store the remainder in the fridge.

Preserved Raspberries

Yield: 1 Cup
Active Time: 10 minutes
Fermenting Time: 2 days
Total Time: 2 days, 10 minutes

Ingredients
1 cup raspberries
½ tsp vegetable starter culture
1 ⅛ cup chlorine-free, filtered water (divided)

Tools
One (8-ounce) fermenting jar with airlock lid
One small bowl

Method
1. Add the raspberries to the fermenting jar. Set to the side.
2. In the small bowl, combine starter culture and 2 tablespoons water. Pour over the raspberries, and top off with the remaining water.
3. Place jar onto a surface that is hidden from direct sunlight, and allow to ferment for up a minimum of 2 days.
4. Store the remainder in the fridge.

Fermented Tomatoes and Tomatillos

Yield: One Quart
Active Time: 10 minutes
Fermenting Time: 5 to 7 days
Total Time: 5 to 7 days, 10 minutes

Ingredients
½ pound grape tomatoes, washed
½ pound tomatillos, husks removed and washed
1 cup 100% pure cane sugar
4 cup chlorine-free, filtered water
1 cup fresh basil, roughly chopped
3 tbsp Himalayan Pink salt

Tools
One (1-gallon) wide-mouth glass jar with lid
One medium saucepan

Method
1. In a medium saucepan, combine sugar, water, and salt. Bring to a boil over medium heat, and immediately remove from the heat. Stir constantly until the sugar is dissolved. Allow to cool to room temperature.
2. In the meantime, poke holes into the tomatoes tomatillos, and pack the jar with tomatoes, tomatillos, and basil. Pour the brine over the tomatoes and tomatillos. Be sure that the tomatoes and tomatillos are fully submerged beneath the brine, but leave about 1 to 2 inches of space from the rim.
3. Place jar onto a surface that is hidden from direct sunlight, and allow to ferment for up a minimum of 5 to 7 days.

4. When ready to serve, enjoy with your favorite dish and store the remainder in the fridge.

Lacto-Fermented Mango and Ginger Chutney

Yield: One Quart
Active Time:
Fermenting Time:
Total Time:

Ingredients
3 cups ripe mangos, peeled and diced
1 small red onion, minced
2 ½ tsp fresh ginger root, minced
2 garlic cloves, minced
¼ cup fresh cilantro, roughly chopped
3 tbsp whey
2 tbsp lemon juice, freshly squeezed
2 tsp curry powder
2 fresh basil leaves, finely chopped
½ tsp crushed red pepper flakes
1 tsp Himalayan Pink salt

Tools
One (1-quart) fermenting jar with airlock lid
One large bowl

Method
1. In the large bowl, combine all of the ingredients and mix well to blend the ingredients.
2. Add to the fermenting jar, and place jar onto a surface that is hidden from direct sunlight, and allow to ferment for up a minimum of 2 to 3 days.
3. Place jar onto a surface that is hidden from direct sunlight, and allow to ferment for up a minimum of 2 days.

4. When ready, enjoy the chutney as desired and store the remainder in the refrigerator.

Berries and Spinach Kraut

Yield: Two Quarts
Active Time: 15 minutes
Fermenting Time: 6 days
Total Time: 6 days, 15 minutes

Ingredients
3 cups spinach, roughly chopped
½ head green cabbage, shredded
½ package kefir whey
1 ½ cup fresh blueberries
1 large shallot
½ cup cranberry juice
1 tbsp Himalayan Pink salt
Chlorine-free, filtered water

Tools
One (2-quart) fermenting jars with airlock lid
One large bowl
One medium bowl

Method
1. In a large bowl, combine cabbage, spinach, shallot, blueberries, and salt. Mix together until the ingredients are well combined. Add the ingredient to the fermenting jar. Pick them tightly inside
2. In a medium bowl, mix together kefir whey and cranberry juice. Mix well until the whey as dissolved and pour over the vegetables in the fermenting jar. Leave about 1 to 2 inches of space in the jar from the rim. Replace the lid.
3. Place jar onto a surface that is hidden from direct sunlight, and allow to ferment for up a minimum of 6 days.

4. Place jar onto a surface that is hidden from direct sunlight, and allow to ferment for up a minimum of 2 days.

Fermented Breads

Dosa

Yield: 4 Cups
Active Time: 5 minutes
Soaking Time: 4 to 6 hours
Fermenting Time: 1 to 2 days
Total Time: 1 to 2 days, 5 minutes

Ingredients
1 cup dry red lentils
1 cup uncooked brown rice
Chlorine-free, filtered water
1 tbsp fenugreek
½ tsp Himalayan Pink salt

Tools
Blender
One large bowl

Method
1. Add rice, lentils, fenugreek and salt to a large bowl. Pour enough water into the bowl so that the ingredients are about 1 to 2 inches beneath the surface. Soak for about 4 to 6 hours.
2. Once the ingredients are done soaking, drain and place into the blender. Blend the ingredients until a smooth consistency is reached. Pour the batter into a large bowl, and allow to ferment on a surface that is hidden from direct sunlight, for a minimum of 1 to 2 days.
3. When ready to enjoy, the dosa batter should be cooked similar to the method of a crepe. Be sure to stir before using.
4. Place remaining batter into the fridge.

Dated Flax Sourdough Bread

Yield: One Loaf
Active Time: 20 minutes
Resting Time: 16 hours
Baking Time: 35 minutes
Total Time: 16 hours, 55 minutes

Ingredients
4 whole dates, pitted and chopped
¼ cup ground flaxseed meal
3 ½ cups white whole-wheat flour
1 cup Sourdough starter, activated and bubbly
1 cup chlorine-free, filtered water
¼ cup organic raw honey
2 tsp Himalayan Pink salt
¼ cup unrefined extra-virgin olive oil

Tools
One large electric mixer, with dough hook, and mixing bowl
One large bowl
One clean kitchen towel
One large baking sheet
Plastic wrap

Methods
1. Add Sourdough starter, water, olive oil, honey, dates, flax, salt, and flour to the large mixing bowl. Mix the ingredients at low speed and process until the dough pulls away from the bowl.
2. Lightly grease the large bowl, and place the dough into the center of the bowl. Place clean towel into some hot water, and place the towel over the bowl.

3. Place bowl onto a surface that is hidden from direct sunlight, and allow the dough to rise for up a minimum of 5 to 7 hours, or until the dough has doubled.
4. Lightly grease the large baking sheet with olive oil. Set to the side.
5. Once the dough is ready, punch the dough down and place the dough onto the prepared baking sheet. Cover with plastic wrap that is coated in oil to keep the dough from sticking to the bread, and leave the dough on the counter to rest for overnight.
6. The follow day, set oven to 400 degrees. And carefully remove the plastic wrap from over the dough.
7. Place the dough into the oven to bake for a minimum of 35 minutes or until the dough is well done. Allow the dough to cool on a cooling rack for about 5 to 10 minutes before serving.

Fermented Beverages

Apple Cider Chia Fresca

Yield: One Quart
Active Time: 5 minutes
Fermenting Time: 10 to 15 minutes
Total Time: 20 minutes

Ingredients
1 tbsp chia seeds
1 cup fresh pineapple chunks
1 cup fresh blueberries
1 cup raspberries
2 tsp apple cider vinegar
4 drops liquid stevia
2 cups purified water

Tools
Blender
One (1-quart) fermenting jar with airlock lid

Method
1. Add the ingredients to the blender and blend until the fruits reach a smooth consistency. Allow the mixture to sit for a minimum of 10 to 15 minutes.
2. Enjoy as desired.

Lacto-Fermented Raspberry Soda

Yield: Two Quarts
Active Time: 10 minutes
Cooking Time: 20 to 30 minutes
Fermenting Time: 3 days
Total Time: 3 days, 40 minutes

Ingredients
4 cups fresh raspberries
1 cup 100% pure cane sugar
½ cup whey
2 cups chlorine-free, filtered water

Tools
Two (1-quart) fermenting jar with airlock lid
One medium saucepan

Method
1. Bring raspberries and sugar to a simmer in the medium saucepan, over medium heat. Allow the raspberry mixture to simmer for a minimum of 20 to 30 minutes. Remove from heat and allow the raspberries to cool.
2. Add the raspberry mixture to each of the fermenting jars along with whey, cover, and place jars onto a surface that is hidden from direct sunlight, and allow to ferment for up a minimum of 3 days.
3. After 3 days remove the raspberry and enjoy your delicious soda. Place the reminder into glass soda bottles store into the refrigerator.

Fermented Orange Juice

Yield: One Quart
Active Time: 10 minutes
Fermenting Time: 2 days
Total Time: 2 days, 10 minutes

Ingredients
2 ½ cups orange juice, freshly squeezed
2 tbsp whey
1 tsp Himalayan Pink salt
1 cup chlorine-free, filtered water

Tools
One (1-quart) fermenting jar with airlock lid

Method
1. Add the orange juice, whey, and salt to the fermenting jar.
2. Add the whey, salt, and water making sure to leave about 1 or 2 inches of space from the rim of the jar.
3. Replace the lid and give the contents of the jar a quick and vigorous shake.
4. Place jar onto a surface that is hidden from direct sunlight, and allow to ferment for up a minimum of 2 days.
5. After the juice is ready, enjoy and place the remainder into the fridge.

Fizzy Fermented Lemonade

Yield: 2 cups
Active Time: 15 minutes
Fermenting Time: 2 days
Total Time: 2 days, 15 minutes

Ingredients
6 large lemons
½ cup 100% pure cane sugar
½ cup whey
2 cups chlorine-free, filtered water

Tools
One (½ -quart) fermenting jar with airlock lid
One manual juicer

Method
1. Juice lemons and pour into the fermenting jar along with sugar, water, and whey.
2. Mix until the whey and sugar is completely dissolved. Cover the jar with the lid.
3. Place jar onto a surface that is hidden from direct sunlight, and allow to ferment for up a minimum of 2 days.
4. After the juice is ready, enjoy and place the remainder into the fridge.

Homemade Kombucha Tea

Yield: One Gallon
Active Time: 1 hour
Fermenting Time: 7 days
Total Time: 7 days, 1 hour

Ingredients
1 SCOBY
2 organic green tea bags
2 organic black tea bags
1 cup 100% pure cane sugar
1 gallon chlorine-free, filtered water

Tools
One (2-gallon) wide-mouth glass jar
One large saucepan
One clean kitchen towel

Method
1. In a large saucepan, bring the gallon of water to a boil. Remove the water from the heat and allow the tea to steep for a minimum of 5 to 10 minutes. Remove the tea bags.
2. Pour the tea into the glass jar, add SCOBY, and cover the jar with the towel, and allow the Kombucha to ferment for a minimum of 7 days.
3. When ready, enjoy Kombucha as desired. Feel free to add ingredients like berries to enhance the taste.

Fermented Dishes

Tomatillo Reuben Sandwich Casserole

Yield: Twelve Servings
Active Time: 15 minutes
Cooking Time: 30 minutes
Total Time: 45 minutes

Ingredients
2 pound Cured Corned Beef, thinly sliced
12 slices Dated Flax Sourdough Bread, cubed
4 cups Tomatillo Sauerkraut, drained and rinsed
1 ½ cup Russian dressing
4 cups Swiss cheese, shredded
Cooking spray

Method
1. Preheat oven to 400 degrees, coat a 9"x13" spray with cooking spray.
2. Distribute bread cubes in a single layer at the bottom of the baking dish, and top with sauerkraut and corned beef. Finish off with dressing. Cover with foil.
3. Bake for 30 minutes and after 20 minutes, remove foil and sprinkle with cheese and bake for 10 minutes or until cheese is melted and bubbly.
4. Serve immediately.

Lemon Berry Cheesecake Bars

Yield: Twelve Bars
Active Time: 15 minutes
Baking Time: 35 minutes
Total Time: 50 minutes

Ingredients
¾ cup fresh or frozen blueberries
1 ¼ cup whole-wheat graham cracker crumbs
1 ½ cup raw almonds, very finely chopped
⅛ cup Moroccan Preserved Lemons
⅛ cup Preserved Raspberries
1 ½ cup 100% pure cane sugar (divided)
32 ounces cream cheese, softened
4 large eggs
¼ cup egg whites
⅓ cup butter, softened
1 tsp lemon extract
1 tsp vanilla extract

Method
1. Set oven to 350 degrees, and coat an 8"x8" baking dish with cooking spray and set aside.
2. Add almonds, graham cracker crumbs, ¼ cup sugar, and butter to a food processor. Pulse until the mixture becomes crumbly, and dump graham cracker mixture into the prepared baking dish. Press the crust down firmly to encourage crust.
3. Place the crust into the oven to bake in the oven for 5 minutes. Remove from oven and set to the side to cool.

4. Using an electric mixer, beat together cream cheese and remaining sugar together in a large bowl. Gradually add eggs, lemon extract, and vanilla extract. Continue to beat until cream mixture is smooth. Gently fold in blueberries, and dump mixture onto graham cracker crust. Evenly distribute and spread with spatula.
5. Bake for 30 to 35 minutes, or until firm mixture is set and firm. Remove from oven and cool on a wire rack for 30 minutes. Cover with plastic wrap and place in fridge to chill for 2 hours.
6. When cheesecake is set, spread an even layer of the lemon preserves over cheesecake and top with the preserved raspberries, cut into 12 bars, and serve immediately.

Pita Chips and Fermented Salsa

Yield: Four Servings
Active Time: 5 minutes
Baking Time: 15 minutes
Total Time: 20 Minutes

Ingredients
4 (6-inch) pitas, split in half horizontally
1 tsp cumin seeds, crushed
1 tsp dried oregano
½ tsp Himalayan Pink salt
2 cups Fiery Fermented Pepper Salsa
Cooking spray

Method
1. Set oven to 375 degrees, and lightly coat a large baking sheet with cooking spray.
2. To prepare chips, coat rough side of each pita half with cooking spray.
3. Sprinkle pita halves evenly with cumin seeds, oregano, and ½ teaspoon salt.
4. Cut each pita half into 8 wedges; arrange wedges in a single layer on baking sheets. Bake in preheated oven for 15 minutes or until golden brown.
5. Serve chips with salsa and enjoy the spiciness!

Flaming Hot Chicken Wings

Yield: Ten Servings
Active Time: 15 minutes
Cooking Time: 50 Minutes
Total Time: 1 hour, 5 Minutes

Ingredients
3 pounds chicken wings, cleaned, tips removed, and wings separated at joints
¼ cup Lacto-Fermented Ketchup
¼ cup Fermented Hot Pepper Sauce
1 tbsp Worcestershire sauce
1 tbsp Dijon mustard
⅓ cup red wine vinegar
4 tbsp unsalted butter
1 tbsp 100% pure cane sugar
1 tsp onion powder
1 tsp garlic powder

Method.
1. Set oven to 450 degrees and line a large rimmed baking sheet with aluminum foil, and coat with cooking spray.
2. In a small saucepan, add fermented ketchup, hot pepper sauce, vinegar, mustard, Worcestershire sauce, onion powder, garlic powder, sugar, and butter. Cook the hot pepper sauce mixture over low heat for a minimum of 10 minutes or until the sauce is warmed, and the sugar is dissolved. Remove the sauce from heat and pour into a small bowl. Set to the side to cool.
3. Once the sauce is cooled, add the wings to a large bowl, and pour ½ cup of the sauce over

the wings. Toss the wings in the bowl to coat
the wings with the sauce.
4. Arrange the wings in an even layer onto the
   prepared baking dish, and brush each with the
   sauce. Roast for 10 minutes, and remove the
   chicken from the oven. Flip over each of the
   wings and brush with more of the sauce.
   Return the wings to the oven to roast for an
   additional 10 minutes.
5. Remove the wings from the oven to flip over
   and brush with more of the sauce, and place in
   the oven to roast for 10 more minutes. Repeat
   this once more.
6. Remove wings to a large bowl and toss with
   reserved sauce. Enjoy the wings with your
   favorite sauce, and side dish.

Savory Sausage Pizza

Yield: Four Servings
Active Time: 10 minutes
Cooking Time: 21 minutes
Total Time: 31 minutes

Ingredients
1 pound Fermented Kosher Apple Salami Sausage, thinly sliced
1 Catalonian Crust
3 tsp cornmeal
3 garlic cloves
¼ cup 100% pure cane sugar
3 cups Fermented Tomatoes and Tomatillos
1 cup ricotta cheese
1 cup mozzarella cheese
1 tsp Himalayan Pink salt
¼ cup unrefined extra-virgin olive oil

Method
1. Set oven to 500 degrees, and lightly grease a 12" pizza pan with olive oil.
2. In a large blender, combine sugar, fermented tomatoes and tomatillos, and garlic. Blend until a smooth consistency is reached. Set to the side.
3. Gently stretch crust into across the prepared pizza pan. Brush the pizza crust with olive oil and sprinkle with cornmeal. Place into the oven to bake for about 5 minutes. Remove from the oven.
4. Spread the puree tomatoes and tomatillos over the crust lean a ½" border. Spread the cheeses in an even layer over the sauce. Arrange the slices of sausage over the cheese.

5. Place the pizza into the oven to bake for a minimum of 16 minutes or until the crust is golden and crispy.

Fermented Smoothies

Berry Kombucha Smoothie

Yield: Two Servings
Active Time: 10 minutes
Blending Time: 2 minutes
Total Time: 12 minutes

Ingredients
1 cup Homemade Kombucha Tea
¾ cup fresh mango, cubed
½ cup blackberries
½ cup blackberries
½ cup raspberries
2 tablespoons chia seeds
1 cup Ice

Method
1. Pour Kombucha into the blender first. Dump all of the ingredients except for the chia seeds into the blender, and puree until all of the ingredients become completely smooth.
2. Pour into your favorite glass, and garnish each serving with 1 tablespoon of chia seeds. Enjoy!

Lemon-Lime Graviola Smoothie

Yield: Two Servings
Active Time: 2 minutes
Blending Time: 3 minutes
Total Time: 5 minutes

Ingredients
½ cup Fizzy Fermented Lemonade
1 cup strawberries, chopped
1 large frozen banana, chopped (peel before freezing)
2 Lime Pickles
½ cup graviola puree
1 large green apple

Method
1. Add the all of the ingredients to the blender and blend for a minimum of 2 to 3 minutes or until the mixture becomes smooth.
2. Pour into two separate serving glasses or enjoy one large serving by yourself!

Berry Kefir Açaí Smoothie

Yield: Two Servings
Active Time: 2 minutes
Blending Time: 6 minutes
Total Time: 8 minutes

Ingredients
2 large frozen bananas, chopped (peel before freezing)
¼ cup açaí puree
½ cup strawberries, chopped
1 cup chilled apricot nectar
1 cup Black and Blue Kefir
2 tbsp lemon juice, freshly squeezed

Method
1. Pour lemon juice, apricot nectar, lemon juice, kefir, and acai puree into the blender. Blend at a low speed for a minimum of 2 to 3 minutes or until the mixture becomes very smooth.
2. Add the bananas and strawberries to the blender and blend for an additional 2 to 3 minutes or until the mixture becomes smooth.
3. Pour into two separate serving glasses or enjoy one large serving by yourself!

Creamy Orange Goji Smoothie

Yield: One Serving
Active Time: 2 minutes
Blending Time: 6 minutes
Total Time: 8 minutes

Ingredients
1 large navel orange, peeled and quartered
¼ cup organic orange juice concentrate
½ cup Fermented Orange Juice
½ cup goji berries
½ cup organic/grass-fed, full-fat ice cream (Vanilla Flavor)
½ cup Probiotic Coconut Yogurt
1 tsp vanilla extract

Method
1. Pour orange juice, orange juice concentrate, ice cream, yogurt, vanilla extract, and goji berries into the blender. Blend at a low speed for a minimum of 2 to 3 minutes or until the mixture becomes very smooth.
2. Add the oranges to the blender and blend for an additional 2 to 3 minutes or until the mixture becomes smooth.
3. Enjoy one large serving by yourself!

Cranberry Noni Smoothie

Yield: Two Servings
Active Time: 2 minutes
Blending Time: 6 minutes
Total Time: 8 minutes

Ingredients
3 tbsp non-pasteurized noni juice
2 large frozen banana, chopped (peel before freezing)
1 cup Cranberry Chutney
½ cup raspberries
¼ cup Moroccan Preserved Lemons
½ cup organic white grape juice
½ cup organic cranberry juice
2 tbsp organic raw honey

Method
1. Pour cranberry juice, grape juice, noni juice, honey, chutney, lemon preserves, and banana into the blender. Blend at a low speed for a minimum of 2 to 3 minutes or until the mixture becomes very smooth.
2. Add the berries to the blender and blend for an additional 2 to 3 minutes or until the mixture becomes smooth.
3. Enjoy one large serving by yourself!

Conclusion

Fermented foods are extremely healthy and carry amazing benefits. It is my hope that the recipes provided in this book will inspire you to incorporate fermented foods into yor everyday life. These recipes are some of the best, and they use some of the best ingredients.

Even though the recipes included in the book work fine the way they are, feel free to add any extra ingredients that you feel would make the recipe taste better or even healthier. Experimentation is always good, but just be sure that you pick the best selection of ingredients when coming up with your own recipe. All flavors don't

Hopefully you have found at least one recipe that you love in this tasty compilation. All of these recipes are suitable for either breakfast, lunch, dinner, or even dessert. These recipes are definitely something that you can prepare to impress yourself, your friends, and family.

CPSIA information can be obtained
at www.ICGtesting.com
Printed in the USA
FSOW03n2147191216
28748FS